T0252709

The ANIMATOR'S SKETCHBOOK

How to **See, Interpret** & **Draw** Like a Master Animator

The **ANIMATOR'S SKETCHBOOK**
by **TONY WHITE**

How to **See, Interpret** & **Draw** Like a Master Animator

CRC Press
Taylor & Francis Group
Boca Raton   London   New York

CRC Press is an imprint of the
Taylor & Francis Group, an **informa** business

A FOCAL PRESS BOOK

CRC Press
Taylor & Francis Group
6000 Broken Sound Parkway NW, Suite 300
Boca Raton, FL 33487-2742

First issued in hardback 2017

© 2017 by Taylor & Francis Group, LLC
CRC Press is an imprint of Taylor & Francis Group, an Informa business

No claim to original U.S. Government works

ISBN 13: 978-1-138-41822-6 (hbk)
ISBN 13: 978-1-4987-7401-7 (pbk)

This book contains information obtained from authentic and highly regarded sources. Reasonable efforts have been made to publish reliable data and information, but the author and publisher cannot assume responsibility for the validity of all materials or the consequences of their use. The authors and publishers have attempted to trace the copyright holders of all material reproduced in this publication and apologize to copyright holders if permission to publish in this form has not been obtained. If any copyright material has not been acknowledged please write and let us know so we may rectify in any future reprint.

Except as permitted under U.S. Copyright Law, no part of this book may be reprinted, reproduced, transmitted, or utilized in any form by any electronic, mechanical, or other means, now known or hereafter invented, including photocopying, microfilming, and recording, or in any information storage or retrieval system, without written permission from the publishers.

For permission to photocopy or use material electronically from this work, please access www.copyright.com (http://www.copyright.com/) or contact the Copyright Clearance Center, Inc. (CCC), 222 Rosewood Drive, Danvers, MA 01923, 978-750-8400. CCC is a not-for-profit organization that provides licenses and registration for a variety of users. For organizations that have been granted a photocopy license by the CCC, a separate system of payment has been arranged.

Trademark Notice: Product or corporate names may be trademarks or registered trademarks, and are used only for identification and explanation without intent to infringe.

Library of Congress Cataloging-in-Publication Data

Names: White, Tony, 1947- author.
Title: The animator's sketchbook : how to see, interpret & draw like a master
animator / Tony White.
Description: Boca Raton : CRC Press, 2016. | Includes bibliographical
references and index.
Identifiers: LCCN 2016016652 | ISBN 9781498774017
Subjects: LCSH: Drawing--Technique. | Animation (Cinematography)
Classification: LCC NC1765 .W475 2016 | DDC 741.5/8--dc23
LC record available at https://lccn.loc.gov/2016016652

Visit the Taylor & Francis Web site at
http://www.taylorandfrancis.com

and the CRC Press Web site at
http://www.crcpress.com

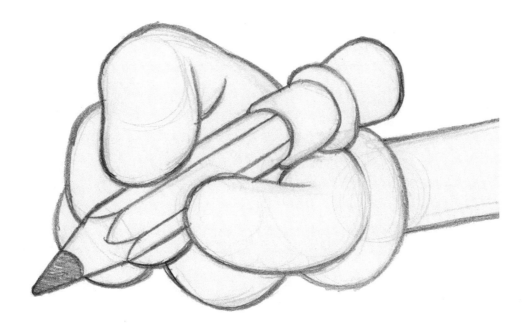

This sketchbook belongs to:

Name _____

Contact _____

(Please return to the above owner in case of loss.)

I dedicate this book to all those master animators of the future who are starting their journey on the long road to animation mastery. Whether you ultimately turn your knowledge to two-dimensional (2D), three-dimensional (3D), stop-motion, or any other form of animation, you will find that the work you put in here will prove the finest foundation you will ever have to grow and learn! Software and generic techniques can be learned by anyone. But the work you create through the Animator's Sketchbook *will be unique to you and you alone. It is, in fact, that special uniqueness that most employers are looking for in this day and age, so don't sell yourself short with the work you do here. A strong understanding of the core principles of movement, based on personal observation and drawing what is seen, really is the key to all animation mastery. I sincerely believe that this book will provide you with that perfect solid ground upon which you can build an outstanding career for yourself. Ultimately, though, this book will only become valuable to you in direct proportion to what you put into it—not me! So I earnestly advise you to give your all to the exercise requirements to be found within the pages of this book—that is, if you really do want to become one of those revered animation masters of the future.*

Tony White

Contents

Part 2   Now It's Time to Draw!

Contents

Part 3   Appendix

Preface

"To the readers of this book - happy sketching!"

Tom Moore

Thank You

To my loving wife, Saille—for loving the person I am instead of the person others would make of me. Your support in everything I try to do (often far too much) is an inspiration to me. Without you, none of it would be at all possible!

Introduction

Draw what you see—not what you think you see!

Imagination is a wonderful thing. From it has come things of great wonder that have brought joy and inspiration to our world. Imagination is the wellspring of all the great books, films, shows, and just about everything else that has moved and entertained us throughout the ages. In more recent times, all of the great animated classics have sprung from that infinite source we call imagination.

As animators especially, imagination is an amazing resource that provides us with so many options in approach that we can take when preparing or conceiving even the shortest of moving sequences. Like an actor on a stage, we need the inspiration of our imagination to guide us in how we portray a character delivering a line or action or performing a powerful emotion to the audience. However, beyond that point—in the actual mechanical creation of the chosen movement—imagination can be our own worst enemy! At this point, we need instead to draw on the reality of the world around us. This is because to realize the performance we have imagined, we need to seriously study and research how that movement works in the real world to perfect our character's actual execution of the actions required.

For example, if we want our character to perform gymnastic somersaults across the floor in an expression of joy or celebration, we don't just do what we imagine it would do. If we did that our action would fall incredibly flat and be unconvincing. Instead, we need to watch gymnasts doing actual flick-flacks across the mat to understand how this action works mechanically. Balance, timing, arcs of action, anticipation, and overlapping action are all elements we can learn from by studying reality. Indeed, it is only by studying that real world around us that we will find those unique little things that will transform our animation to a higher level, whatever form of animation we execute. We merely have to train our eyes to *see* these things—and then apply them to our animation technique—which is what this sketchbook is all about!

So this book is all about the process of *seeing, recording,* and *interpreting* through drawing. It is through this process of observing and sketching that you will open to yourself a whole world of new understanding and expression that your mind can barely imagine. Watching in slow motion a sequence of an athlete, juggler, actor, or even everyday people walking about doing their business will reveal subtleties of pose, action, and timing that we cannot possibly visualize until we see it in action. The simple experience of studying people drinking coffee in Exercise 2 will immediately show us the various ways that people actually hold a cup or place their bodies. These variations alone will each tell their own story simply by capturing the poses that people adopt!

Therefore, do not take the observation and drawing challenges of this book lightly. Everything you attempt here is designed to open your eyes and teach you new things. Your imagination will set the stage, but your observation and drawings along these lines will dictate the performance. It is only by doing this that you will be fully able to push your animation to levels that the master animators of the past achieved. Look, learn, and draw—these are the foundations of what will make you a master animator too!

Part 1
What This Book Is All About

The Importance of Drawing

It must be stated right up front that *The Animator's Sketchbook* is *not* a book that teaches you how to draw. That's something you'll hopefully have learned already—or if not, something you should consider more seriously. You don't need to be able to draw like Rembrandt or Leonardo da Vinci, of course. But it is extremely valuable for any creative person to know their way around a pencil—even if they work in CG or another nondrawing animated discipline eventually. The "humble pencil" is the finest hardware ever created to express an idea or put down a concept for later development. Indeed, pretty much most creations tend to begin with a simple pencil sketch or thumbnail scribble at the start of their conception. So master animators of the future, you neglect the power of the pencil at your own risk!

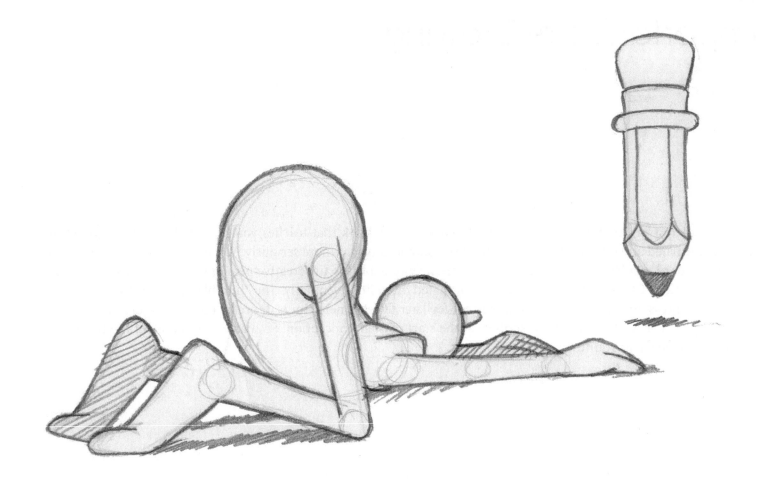

What This Book Will and Won't Do

What *The Animator's Sketchbook will* do is point you in the right direction to *see* the information you most need to see and understand as an emerging animator. We live in a world of perpetual visual stimulus, but perhaps we often can't see the forest for the trees when we look. So here you will find 66 exercises that will open your eyes to the moving world that is all around you. Then—perhaps the most revolutionary thing of all—*The Animator's Sketchbook* is a book that actually requires you to *draw in it* as you read.

The Animator's Sketchbook won't tell you *how* you should draw—at least in terms of a drawing style. You will be expected to draw figures pretty much all the time, but the style and technique you adopt to do those drawings are entirely your decision. What is recommended, however, is that you draw in a style that is quick and you use a technique that can be worked with quickly and consistently. Many of the exercises in *The Animator's Sketchbook* need to be sketched within a minimal amount of time, so you'll definitely need to be able to draw them quickly but accurately. Speed, continuity, and clarity are definitely your biggest allies when it comes to arriving at a drawing that you are comfortable with.

How This Book Is Structured

I'm sure you will have seen that most textbooks on animation are packed full with text and illustrations that cover most of the aspects of the animation process—the author's own books included. Traditional sketchbooks, on the other hand, are entirely devoid of anything except blank pages. *The Animator's Sketchbook* positions itself somewhere in between these two extremes. It is done in this way so you will learn the core foundations of pose and movement through brief written guidelines as you use the additional blank spaces on each page to sketch out what you are required to observe and draw. In this unique way, *The Animator's Sketchbook* offers itself up as a definitive, foundational workbook for students who wish to become master animators or for current professional animators (of every kind) who want to raise the bar on their own mastery accordingly.

Illustration Pages

On the page that follows most of the dedicated drawing and instruction pages you will find grayed-out images that illustrate the nature of the exercise you are about to attempt. If you choose to, you can draw over these in your own style, in a way to become more familiar with the challenge you are about to take on. Alternatively, you can use the blank pages as extra drawing opportunities instead, i.e., where you can add more of your own original gesture drawings to supplement the drawing exercises you will be doing anyway. This is probably the preferred thing to do, as at the end of everything you will want to show your completed sketchbook, featuring as many of your own drawings as you can, when you pitch your animation show reel at important interviews. Clearly, the more drawings you pack into its every available drawing space, the more impressive it will be for you in the eyes of that important hiring person.

12) Next it is important to look at emotions and body language. As we all know, people at a funeral or memorial service often tend to look extremely sad. 'Sad' is what we're now looking for. So, select 4 examples of people looking sad, especially by way of their body language, and sketch a gesture drawing of each onto the page opposite. Chose your pose positions well, remembering especially what you've learned about silhouetting in the previous exercise. (Take no more than 3 minutes to complete each sketch.)

Claire Fritz/Student.

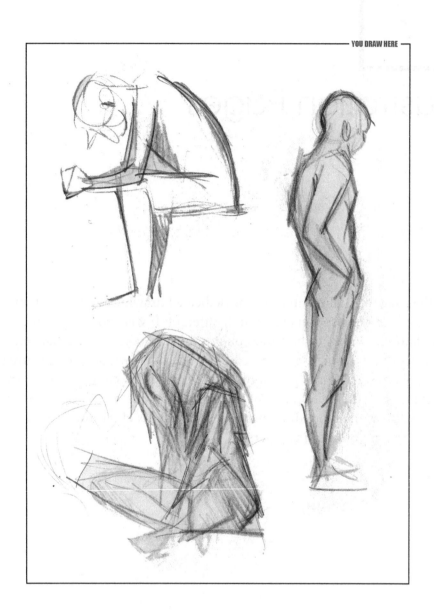

The Process

The process of using *The Animator's Sketchbook* is very simple. On almost all of opening pages of each exercise, you will find brief written guidelines that will help you to see and draw specific things that you need to observe as an animator. You will be directed to specific actions or locations that you need to find and draw. There will be a time limit given for each instruction too, so you will have to learn to discipline yourself in doing the exercise in the time required. When you have completed all the drawing assignments in this book—and hopefully added many of your own too—you should have an immaculate, animation-focused sketchbook that will be a major part of your presentation material when you go out to work in the industry. There will of course be nothing like it out there—it will be entirely unique to you. This will hopefully put you ahead of your competition in any job or college position you apply for.

Simple Is Best

Once upon a time, a Pixar recruiter announced that if a kid came through the door who couldn't draw, but presented them with the most beautifully animated stick figure animation imaginable, they would hire him immediately. They explained that in a world where a knowledge of computers, software, and technology was the norm among student graduates these days, the hardest thing for them to find was those student animators who knew how to move things well, i.e., according to the foundational principles of motion that have been laid down by the great animators of the past.

In this context, it didn't matter how well a person drew of course—just that he could demonstrate what he knew with the skills he had. This book encourages that. The quality or finish of your actual drawings in *The Animator's Sketchbook* is not as important as the knowledge and understanding that they are reflecting. Even if you really can only draw stick figures, it's OK as long as you make sure that the poses and principles you are representing with them accurately reflect the pose or gesture you have observed. This is why *simple really is best* when it comes to how you approach the drawings you create in your sketchbook. You may well be able to draw like the finest old masters who have ever lived. But if your drawings don't tell the story of what you have observed, then they will mean nothing in terms of your animation progression.

Introducing Arnie

To illustrate most of the exercise text in this book, I have used the simplest of simple illustrative characters—Arnie—to demonstrate the essence of what is being said. Arnie has been with me on my animation and teaching journey for a long time now. He is so easy to understand and draw that I find he's a huge asset for student animators especially. Animation beginners are often overwhelmed by the complexity of the principles of movement they need to know—let alone drawing a character that represents them. So by offering such a simple teaching form to them, it makes everything else they are attempting to learn and demonstrate so much easier.

Consequently, if you're comfortable with drawing Arnie for your drawing exercises in this book, then by all means do so. I can only repeat that it is not the quality or the design of your drawings that matters here, but what you do with those designs. Arnie has been tried and tested over the years as a great vehicle to represent the principles of movement, so it could make your life considerably easier if you adopt him for your own gesture drawing exercises. If, on the other hand, you do feel a strong need to create a character of your own to work with, then that is great too. Just make sure that whatever character design you finally decide upon is fast and easy to draw, as the exercises that follow will often have strict and demanding time limits attached to them.

(Note: You will find a useful turnaround model sheet of Arnie in the Appendix section at the back of this book. Accompanying that you will find additional exercises on how to design and create your own character too. It will be of great benefit to you if you work through these Appendix exercises before you do anything else, as these exercises will help you significantly in fully familiarizing yourself with whatever character design you finally go with before taking on the core pose and gesture assignments to be found throughout this book.)

The Key Pose Animation Process

For those new to animation, it might help to explain a little about the basic approach—specifically the basic key pose animation process. Most animation is made up of *key poses, breakdown positions*, and *inbetweens*. However, the most important among all of these is the key poses. If you don't get your key poses right, then no amount of finessing, rendering, or special effecting will ever make your animation right. This book deals primarily with the art of key poses, i.e., the art of seeing and interpreting them in real-life activities. Key poses (alternatively known as keys or key positions) are best defined as *identifiable changes of direction, action, or emphasis within a particular sequence of movement*. The better we can identify and implement these key poses, the better our animation will become. Every *master animator* has to learn how to observe the key moments in the actions of people, animals, or animate objects if their animation is to truly come alive and be convincing. For example, if a person is hammering a nail into a wall, the first key pose might be with the hammer up, about to strike. It will then move back toward another key pose that prepares for the hit, and finally, the last key pose of the hammer actually hitting the nail will be established. There will of course be more of these, but these three will aptly illustrate the point for now. A master animator will understand the required key poses of an action in their mind, if they don't, they will go out and study a similar action in the real world and make visual, reference sketches to enable them to understand the action better. This is precisely the approach this book takes and how you too will learn how to think and see like a master animator. (Note: For a more in-depth understanding of the much wider principles and processes of animation, read the author's previous books on the subject—a list of which can be found at the back of this publication.)

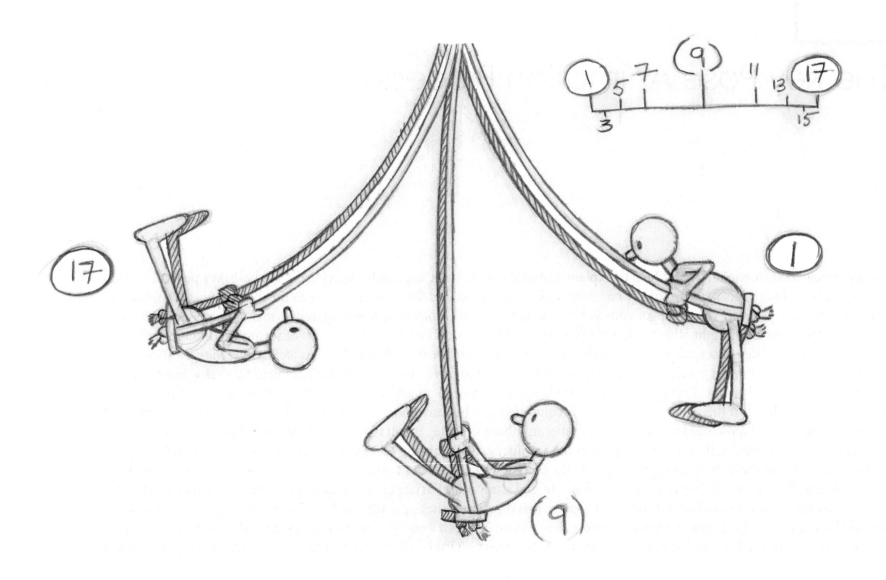

Gesture Drawings vs. Thumbnails

Throughout this book, you will be asked to produce either gesture drawings or thumbnail sketches. So, let us define what these are before you start.

Gesture Drawings

A gesture drawing is essentially a fast, observational sketch where the artist is looking, interpreting, and drawing what he sees before him. *Speed drawing* is another term for these, if you like—although the drawings still have to be accurate even if they are drawn quickly. Gesture drawings for animation purposes can even be an *exaggeration* of what is seen—as long as these exaggerations (or caricatures) are accurately reflective of what is seen and not just bad drawings. A gesture drawing is wholly concerned with the observer looking analytically at the pose or position of a character (or object) in front of him and then drawing speedily what he actually sees (as opposed to what he thinks he sees). Therefore, gesture drawings are a fundamentally important weapon in an animator's armory.

Thumbnail Drawings

In other parts of the book, you will be asked to create quick, imaginary, small-sized concept sketches of things you need to conceive or think up. These are called thumbnail drawings. Thumbnail drawings (also known as thumbs or thumbnails) are effectively a very quick scribble, sketch, or doodle that gets an initial idea down on paper ahead of further study or research taking place. These are therefore not final sketches, or even observational gesture drawings in any way. They are more a *stream of consciousness* kind of thing, where you brainstorm your thoughts and get them down as quickly as possible. They are effectively the foundational basis upon which all future work is based, which is why many animators "thumb out" their animation ideas before fully commiting them to paper or computer.

PART 2
Now It's Time to Draw!

Exercise 1

Anticipation

As a warm-up, let's explore the notion of anticipation. With any main animated action there's almost invariably a moment just preceeding it when the movement goes in the opposite direction. For example, if a character jumps into the air, there is often a move (anticipation) downward before he or she jumps upward. This applies to most of our real-world actions to some extent, which will need to be exaggerated significantly in animation if it is to work convincingly. This exaggeration is particularly notice-able in classical cartoon animation, especially traditional Warner Brothers animation. Therefore, for this first exercise you should study and draw an appropriate pose for a real person about to hammer a nail into a piece of wood. When you have done this, observe what happens just before he or she hits the nail. Draw that position next to the first one on the next blank page. *(Take no more than 2–3 minutes to complete both drawings.)*

Exercise 2

Posture

For our second drawing exercise let's explore variations in posture. Find a popular coffee bar and observe everyone drinking their drinks. Note how although each person is effectively doing the same thing, their method—or posture—will be different as they do it. So, on the next blank page sketch 4 different pose positions of the people you are observing. If no suitable coffee bar is available for you to draw in, select any kind of public location where people are drinking. Exaggerate the pose positions if it helps you express the differences better—as a good animator would! *(Take no more than 2–3 minutes per pose drawing.)*

Exercise 3

Physical Exercise

Now you have some idea of what a gesture drawing is all about, select 4 different people doing some kind of physical exercise. They might be digging, washing a car, sweeping the floor, etc.—whatever it is that makes them active. Draw your 4 people poses on the next blank page. *(Take no more than 2–3 minutes per drawing to do this.)*

(Note: Your temptation in this and all the following action assignments will be to use a photograph or freeze a moment in time on a video to base your gesture drawing on. Try not to do this as the photographic lens can both distort and flatten any image it is capturing. Its far better to use "live" activities to train your eye with, as these will give you a far better idea of the shape, form, volume, and depth of what you're looking at. As a second choice, go to moving video on Vimeo, YouTube, etc., and only as a final resort use a photograph.)

Exercise 4

Sporting Observation

By now you should be feeling more confident with sketching gesture drawings from observation—and maybe even beginning to train your inner "animator's eye" to capture moving moments in time. So next observe serious sports men and women in competition. From their dynamic movements choose 4 extreme, defining poses and draw them on the next blank page. *(Take no more than 2 minutes per drawing.)*

Exercise 5

Single-Person Action

Instead of selecting several different people doing different things, this time pick a single person executing several things in one complete action sequence. This suggests that you could remain in a sports environment showing a progression of action, or else someone going through the stages of an everyday chore. Sketch 4 gesture drawings that define different aspects of the sequence you're observing. *(Take no more than 2 minutes per pose drawing.)*

Exercise 6

Two-Person Observation

Pushing your gesture drawing observational skills a little further, we will now employ the scenario of two or more individuals interacting with each other. On the next blank page, sketch 4 separate gesture drawings that define their unfolding relationship with each other. These can be friendly poses, as with kids playing. They could be lovers in a park, walking hand in hand. They might even be more adversarial, such as two opponents in a boxing ring. Your challenge is to capture the give-and-take of their relationship as best you can. *(Take no more than 5 minutes to do each drawing.)*

Exercise 7

Pose and Silhouette

It might help to share another golden rule with you now. It is not enough to just create a great pose position. Experienced artists and animators all know that to maximize the visual impact of a posed image, it needs to be staged in such a way that the viewer will immediately see the story it's trying to communicate. Communication in animated action especially is everything. Therefore, "silhouetting" is something that is extremely valuable to you. Silhouetting effectively means that if you choose to shade in your character pose black, then the silhouette it makes should still explain the story of the pose you have drawn completely. Hands, arms, and legs especially should be set away from the body in your poses, to make its silhouette stronger. To understand this fully, draw at the top of the next blank page these two versions of a character holding an apple. Compare the difference. Now shade in second versions of them both below and compare the difference from a silhouette point of view. *(Take as long as you need to complete this exercise.)*

Exercise 8

Held Object with *Good* Silhouette

Now find a person from life who you can direct and then observe. Ask her to hold an apple, small ball, or similar object, out in front of her. Position yourself so you can see the most clear silhouetted position you can and make a gesture drawing of it. *(Take no more than 3 minutes to complete this drawing.)*

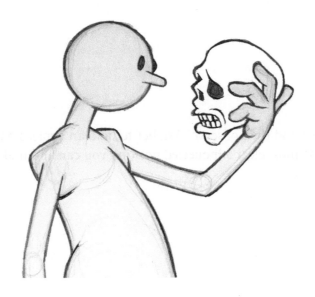

Exercise 9

Held Object with *Poor* Silhouette

Using the same person and pose as the previous exercise, position yourself so that the apple—or object that is being held by the character—is positioned directly between you and the person who is posing. Create a new gesture drawing of this. *(Take no more than 3 minutes to complete each drawing.)*

Exercise 10

Blacked-in Silhouettes

Finally, outline copies of both of the previous apple drawings and black them in to test the silhouettes they make. Compare the two. *(Take as long as you like to complete this exercise.)*

Exercise 11

Pose Alternatives

Every picture tells a story. It is important to remember that no animation will work successfully unless you know how to present it in a way that best tells the story. We know that most movies tell a story, as that is the essence of narrative filmmaking. However, animated storytelling must go much farther than this. Scenes within a film need to tell their own individual stories too. Actions within each scene also have to tell their own story. Even poses within an action must tell their own story if that action is to be convincing. Consequently, if you are not able to sketch gesture drawings that tell stories, then you will really struggle to animate well. As they say, the pose is everything. So this time, pick any of the action drawings you have drawn on the previous pages and use your imagination to conceive 4 new ways of expressing it. Sketch your 4 new ideas onto the next blank page. *(Take no more than 3 minutes to do this.)*

Exercise 12

Emotions and Body Language: Sad

Next, it is important to look at emotions and body language. As we all know, people at a funeral or memorial service often tend to look extremely sad. Sad is what we're now looking for. So, select 4 examples of people looking sad, especially by way of their body language, and sketch a gesture drawing of each on the next blank page. Choose your pose positions well, remembering especially what you've learned about silhouetting in the previous exercise. *(Take no more than 3 minutes to complete each sketch.)*

Exercise 13

Emotions and Body Language: Happy

Now by contrast, find a social gathering or public group that is displaying clear happiness and sketch 4 examples of people in happy poses. Again, facial information is not nearly as important as body language in these gesture drawings. *(Take no more than 2 minutes to complete each drawing.)*

Exercise 14

Emotions and Body Language: Transitions

Now reflecting your previous sad and happy drawings, sketch a series of 4 transitioning positions from sad to happy. Do all 4 drawings in sequence on the next blank page. Your gesture drawings here will need to be the product of your imagination—unless of course you can find a friend or colleague who will pose the changing positions for you to draw. *(Take no more than 3 minutes to complete each drawing.)*

Exercise 15

Balance

Something that is not dealt with in most animation teaching books—or even online tutorials—is balance. Balance is a fundamental aspect of biped pose creation in particular. It took me a decade or more as a professional animator to fully recognize this principle, although once I'd got it, my work elevated to an entirely new level! Effectively, balance means that with any two-legged character moving, its center of gravity *has* to be over its point, or points, of contact with the ground. This effectively means that if it's walking and both feet are on the ground at the same time—as in a stride position—the main weight of its body *has* to be located somewhere above the two feet positions. Alternatively, if only one foot is on the ground at any moment in time, then the body weight *has* to be above the foot that's on the ground. So, look at this generic walking sequence and sketch on the next blank page 2 of the poses within it that represent the principles of balance mentioned above. *(Take no more than 3 minutes to complete each drawing.)*

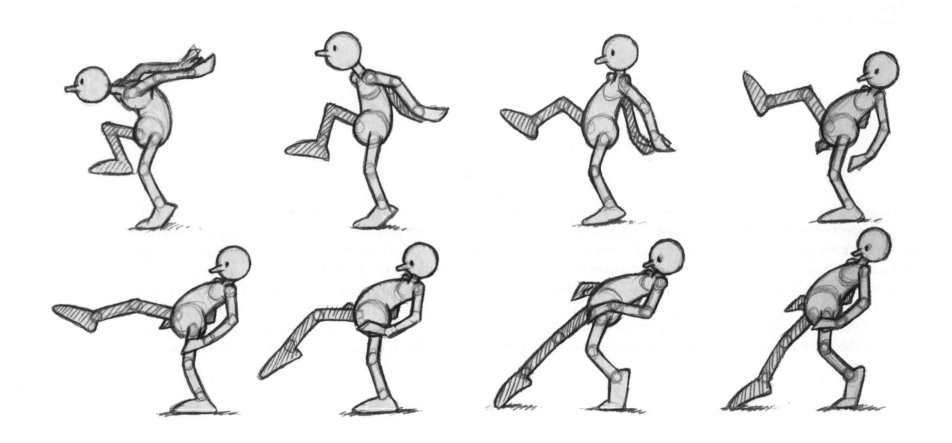

Exercise 16

Human Balance

Open Google Images and type in the search term "human balance." Review what comes up and then select 4 images that you feel most represent the principle of balance (i.e., the body mass is positioned over a single point, or points, of contact with the ground). Sketch out a gesture drawing for each of these on the next blank page. *(Take no more than 3 minutes to complete each drawing.)*

The Animator's Sketchbook

Plate 76. Human Balance.

Exercise 17

Balance with Weight

Observing people carrying heavy loads can shed further light on the nature of balance. For example, watch the different ways a shopper holds his body when (i) going into a store and (ii) coming out of it. Going in, he will pretty much walk normally. But coming out—laden with heavy shopping bags—he will adjust his body lean significantly to compensate for the additional weight over his feet. Therefore, draw 2 gesture drawings on the next blank page that indicate the before and after of carrying a weight. Attempt to dramatize the differing nature of these 2 poses for maximum effect. *(Take no more than 3 minutes to complete each drawing.)*

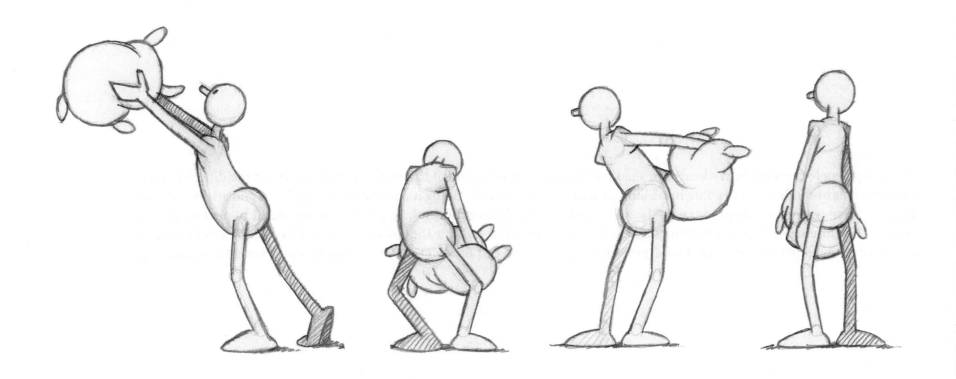

Exercise 18

Weight Shifts in Walks

If you study people walking from the front, you will note that they sway their body mass from side to side as they attempt each stride. This is another example of character balance in action. It is only when our weight is balanced over our contact foot that our free one can be lifted and brought through to make the next stride. Indeed, the larger or heavier a person is, the more likely she is to shift her weight from side to side even further. So, sketch out 4 gesture drawings on the next blank page, showing the shift of body mass as she walks. A view from the front or back will make this more evident. *(Take no more than 2 minutes to complete each drawing.)*

Exercise 19

Weight and Body Stance

As I hope you will have noticed already, there is a significant difference in the body stance of a person who is carrying a heavy weight and one who is not. The character carrying the weight will adjust his pose (and therefore his balance) to compensate. So find your own 2 examples of a person carrying a weight and not carrying a weight. When you have, sketch a gesture drawing for each—side by side—on the next blank page to show the difference between them. *(Take no more than 3 minutes to complete each drawing.)*

Exercise 20

Balance and Dance

Finally on balance. Study a dance sequence where a person is significantly moving their body weight from one foot to the other, such as in ballet, modern dance, or something similar. Identify 4 poses within that sequence where the balanced body shapes are very different and the center of gravity is always directly over their foot's point of contact with the floor. *(Take no more than 2 minutes to complete each drawing.)*

Exercise 21

Form

When animating in a traditional hand-drawn animation style—or even blocking out poses for any other style of animation—one of the most difficult things to do is to keep the form consistent. Maintaining shape, proportions, and volume with any multiple drawings of the same character is difficult for anyone. Try the following yourself and see how good you are at it. *(Taking no more than 3 minutes to execute each of the following drawings.)*

1. Take a toy or a doll and draw it from one angle in the top left-hand quarter of the next blank page.
2. Next, turn the toy 90% and draw it again in the top-right quadrant.
3. Again, turn it another 90% and draw it this time in the bottom-left quadrant.
4. Finally, turn it 90% once more and draw it in the bottom-right quadrant. Now measure the various proportions and volumes from drawing to drawing as best you can. If there is little variation, you're a "master of form." However, it is most likely that you won't be that, so the following exercises will help.

Exercise 22

Bouncing Ball

Start simply with this bouncing ball exercise. At the peak of its bounce, a standard rubber ball will retain a perfectly spherical shape. However, after it descends and hits the ground, it will deform into a flatter, "squash" shape. Yet when it's either ascending or descending, the ball will tend to adopt a longer, narrower "stretch" position. So, take a decorative ball and on the next blank page sketch all 3 modes of it bouncing: perfectly spherical, squashed, and stretched. Ensure that the overall size and volume within the ball are consistent from drawing to drawing. If you have space on the page, repeat this exercise more than once. *(Take no more than 2 minutes to complete each drawing.)*

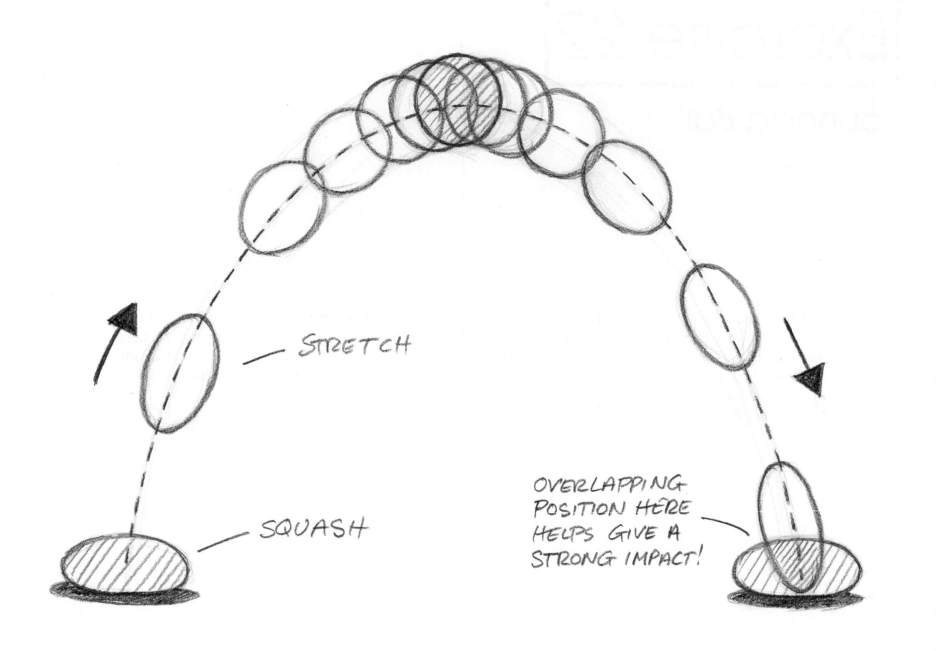

STRETCH

SQUASH

OVERLAPPING POSITION HERE HELPS GIVE A STRONG IMPACT!

Exercise 23

Squash and Stretch

Non-cartoon (i.e., anatomically based) animation will require you to apply the same squash and stretch distortion principles as with the bouncing ball; however, for this you'll need to achieve it by working with the actual anatomy of the character, rather than distorting it as if it were made of rubber. To achieve this, you need to sketch a (say) jumping realistic figure through 3 modes of action: static, squashing, and stretching. This realistically means sketching first a standing figure, and then one with the knees bent and the body leaning forward slightly, in preparation for a jump, and finally, one where the figure is reaching up vertically, off the ground, at the height of the jump. Use a real-world reference for this if you can, and exaggerate the poses to provide a stronger, more dramatic effect. *(Take no more than 3 minutes to complete each drawing.)*

1   2   3   4   5   6   7   8   9

The Animator's Sketchbook

Exercise 24

Rotating Observational Point

Training your eye to appreciate form from every angle is really important to the modern animator, who more often than not deals with 3 dimensions, rather than 2. To help you do this, find a partner who is willing to pose for you. Sketch them first from a profile view. Then, circle around him in approximate 20-degree increments, sketching him from each new angle. Keep this process going until you have sketched him from an entire 360-degree viewpoint, making sure that at each time you are maintaining the proportions and volume of his head and body consistently throughout. *(Take no more than 5 minutes to complete each drawing.)*

(Note: If you want to really test the consistency of your form from drawing to drawing, film each sketch for 24 frames on a suitable video camera and then play back the video. Your drawings will appear to rotate, indicating quite clearly how well you have kept the consistency of form from beginning to end.)

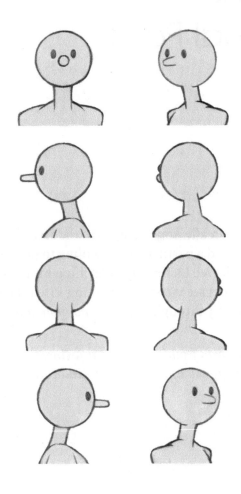

Exercise 25

Form Consistency

It is extremely important that you achieve *form consistency* when research sketching. To experience this, observe someone playing tennis and then draw on the next blank page 4 different gesture drawings from different moments within the action. As you do so, pay as much attention to maintaining a consistent bodily form as you do to recording the person's actual physical pose positions. *(Take no more than 3 minutes to complete each drawing.)*

Exercise 26

Rotating Objects

Sometimes it is solid objects that need to be animated through a moving sequence, not bipedal bodies. So, follow the process of Exercise 24, but instead of drawing a posing figure, this time draw a solid object from around a 360-degree viewpoint. Your object could be a box, a car, or even a building. As long as it contains rigid, static shapes that you can draw from a 360-degree viewpoint, all is good. Again, work at keeping the core shape and form consistent throughout. *(Take between 2 and 5 minutes to complete each drawing, depending on its complexity.)*

Exercise 27

Sequential Action

Animation is all about sequential action, and good sequential action is all about flow, placement, and timing. It therefore helps to study sequential action in real life to make the whole process clearer in your mind before attempting animation. This kind of visual research is so important to an animator, as no two people ever move in exactly the same way, even if they are doing precisely the same action. A walking action is a good example of this. Generically, everyone walks the same way—one leg in front of the other, with arms opposing. However, if you really look hard at the way people walk, you'll see slight variations in their movements. This can be a result of such factors as bodily limitations, mood, intention, and environmental or even weather-induced forces acting upon them. So, observe people walking in the street and sketch 4 different gesture drawings that epitomize the way they are walking. Exaggerate where necessary to make a point. *(Take no more than 3 minutes to create each drawing.)*

The Animator's Sketchbook

Exercise 28

Cup and Hand

Now something that is very simple and accessible to stage. Observe your nondrawing hand resting on the desk. Lift it from its starting position, grab a cup that's farther away, bring the cup toward you, and then finally place it down on the desk just a little nearer than where your hand originally started. It's a simple action, but if you break it down into a minimum of 8 gesture drawings, you'll see that this simple piece of sequential action contains more underlying movements and shifts of planes than you could possibly have imagined. For example, note the angles of the cup as the hand picks it up and moves it toward you, as well as the curved paths of action that your hand and the cup define as they moves from beginning to end. *(Take no more than 2 minutes to complete each drawing.)*

Exercise 29

Object Throw

A really impressive piece of sequential action can be seen when a person is fast-throwing an object. Generally, they will hold the object in their hand, draw back their arm in readiness to throw, unleash the throw with their maximum effort (often leading from the shoulder, then the elbow, then the wrist, and finally the hand), follow through with their arm around the body when they have released the object, and then return to a standing position to observe where the object has landed. For this exercise, therefore, study the movement of a baseball pitcher or a javelin thrower, and create 6 gesture drawings that define the critical moments in that sequence. *(Take no more than 2 minutes to complete each drawing.)*

Exercise 30

Generic Walk

Now returning to the walking action mentioned earlier. When a person walks generically, they will pretty much adopt the poses indicated on this page. Study this sequential action of two walk strides and familiarize yourself with it. Next, go out into a public place and sketch individuals you see as they walk by. Allocate a different person's pose for each of the 9 positions you see in this sequence. (The first and last are the same.) After you've completed all 9 drawings, film them one after another, holding them for 4 frames each if you can, and play back the video. This should give you a quite accurate, albeit slightly surreal, generic walking action. *(Take no more than 2 minutes to complete each drawing.)*

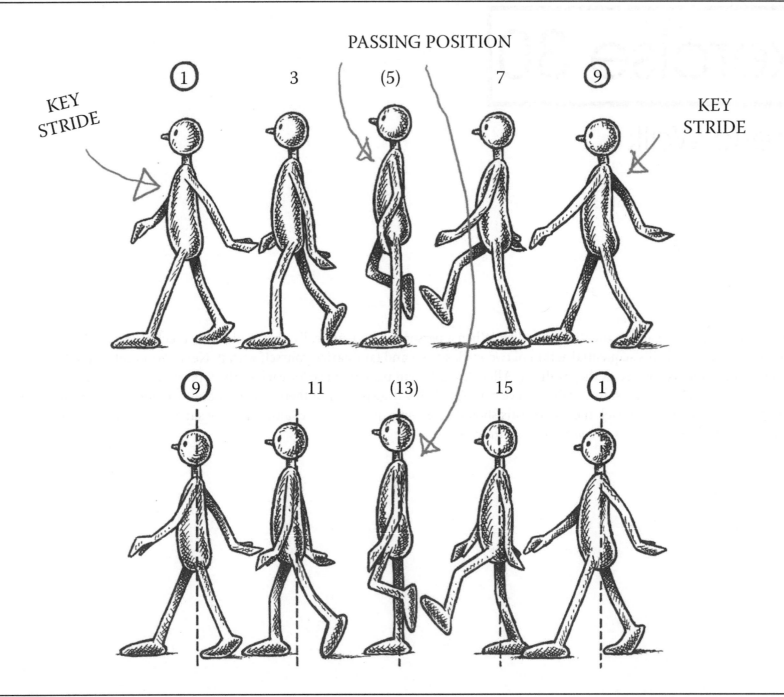

PASSING POSITION

KEY STRIDE

1 3 (5) 7 9

KEY STRIDE

9 11 (13) 15 1

Exercise 31

Bird Flight

Bird flight is more than just the bird moving straight wings up and down. There is, in fact, a very complex process of sequential action going on—founded on the anatomy of the bird in question. So study the video of a bird flying (in slow motion, if possible) and produce a minimum of 5 gesture sketches that define that action. If possible, also study the skeletal anatomy of the bird in question, which will indicate just how and why the wings move as they do. *(Take no more than 4 minutes to complete each drawing.)*

Exercise 32

Breakdown Positions

Return to your previous sequential drawings of a person throwing an object. Using these drawings, visualize and sketch on the next blank page how an inbetween drawing might look midway between each of your key positions. (Note: Quite often an inbetween position is not entirely that, as parts of the body move farther or faster than others—known in animation terms as the 'successive breaking of joints'. Study your original reference footage to see what is happening in the midpoints of the particular pose sequence you have drawn.) If possible, trace every drawing separately in the middle of its own sheet of paper. Then videotape each drawing sequentially, holding them for 4 frames each. When playing the video back, you'll get an instant appreciation of how the overall action is working and what that many drawings means when played back in real time on a video screen. *(Take no more than 1 minute to complete each drawing.)*

The Animator's Sketchbook

Exercise 33

Achieving Weight

Weight is essential to creating good animation, and there are ways of applying the illusion of weight that will improve significantly the quality of animated movement. The effects of gravity (and therefore weight) can exert a significant effect on the way characters move or are posed. Weight pulls down on everything that exists in this world—often in the sense that they become shorter, slower, droopier, or more stooped. The effects of weight can also slow action down too. Therefore, *before* you observe real-world situations, use the next blank page to draw a number of thumbnail sketches that imply gravity affecting people and things. This is a random, stream-of-thought, brainstorming kind of thing, so don't get too serious. As long as your thumbs suggest weight or the effects of weight on things, all will be good. Fill up the page with as many drawn ideas as you can. *(Take no more than 1 minute per sketch.)*

Exercise 34

Thin People

Now go outside and observe 4 very thin, light people who are moving normally. On the next blank page, sketch gesture drawings of each them, indicating their absence of weight. *(Take no more than 2 minutes to complete each drawing.)*

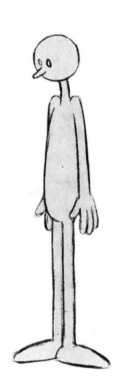

Exercise 35

Heavy People

Now by comparison, observe 4 very broad and heavy people and draw on the next blank page gesture drawings that define their bulk and weight. These should of course contrast greatly with your previous drawings of the lighter people. *(Take no more than 2 minutes to complete each drawing.)*

Exercise 36

Weight Carry

Next, study an individual who is carrying a significant weight—i.e., a man carrying a sack; a mother, a child; or a kid, a heavy toy—and sketch, on the next blank page, 4 separate gesture drawings of each. You are attempting here to show how they physically compensate for the weight they are carrying, so push your poses accordingly. And don't forget what you learned about the use of balance, specifically the center of gravity needing to be over one or both feet if the character is standing. *(Take no more than 3 minutes to complete each drawing.)*

Exercise 37

Nonobservational Drawing

Now, using *only* your imagination, on the next blank page draw 4 thumbnail sketches of the 4 individuals you featured in Exercise 34 carrying the 4 individuals you featured in Exercise 35. Here you really have to apply exaggeration and caricature to communicate the visual story you are trying to communicate. But again, don't neglect the element of balance at the same time. *(Take no more than 3 minutes to complete each drawing.)*

The Animator's Sketchbook

Exercise 38

Moving with Weight

The last exercise with weight. Draw on the next blank page 4 gesture drawings that depict different individuals trying to push, pull, or otherwise move objects that are either too heavy to be moved or are resisting being moved at all. This should be based solely on observation—yet could be one of those rare occasions where you can resort to photographic reference material found on the Internet. *(Take no more than 3 minutes to complete each drawing.)*

Exercise 39

Framing

It is not just drawing a pose or a gesture dynamically that maximizes the impact of an image or its animation. Framing, i.e., just *how* you place your pose, gesture, or animation within the screen frame to ensure its maximum effect, is very important too. What helps is breaking up the screen format into thirds. In other words, if you place your main foreground object or character upon one of the vertical third line positions, you'll find that, aesthetically, the shot is far more pleasing and impactful on the eye. It will more naturally draw the audience's eye to it if you do so. Similarly, the same can apply to your background landscape material. If you place your environment's horizon line on the upper or lower third division line, then it will give a far more dramatic effect to everything. For example, placing the horizon line on the lower third division line will tend to give the foreground object more height, or a sense of looking up on things. Alternatively, placing the horizon line on the upper third line will conversely make the foreground subject feel somewhat smaller and as if we are looking down on it. This can give a strong psychological message to the audience if we consciously work with it. So for this exercise, draw thumbnail sketches of some of your favorite paintings, photographs, or images that conform to the third rule. Fill the next blank page with your thumbnail sketches, providing yourself with a valuable archive of framing approaches that inspire you. *(Take no more than 2 minutes to complete each thumbnail.)*

Exercise 40

Landscape: Vertical Framing

More proactively, go outside and find for yourself a landscape view that has a vertical foreground object in it. Sketch 3 gesture drawing versions of this on the next blank page. One requires the vertical object to be in the center of the frame. One should have it placed on the right-side third division line. The final view needs to be placed on the left-side third division line. These drawings don't need to be too detailed—just distinct enough to differentiate the foreground from the background. Consider them all and reflect on the merits, or not, of each. Make notes on the page if it helps you remember what you are noticing. *(Take no more than 4 minutes to complete each drawing.)*

Exercise 41

Landscape: Horizontal Framing

Now find a similar view and sketch 3 gesture drawing versions of this. One should have the horizon line in the middle of the frame. Another should have the horizon line on the upper third division line. The last should have the horizon on the lower third division line. Review the three drawings and consider the merits, or not, of each. Make notes on the page if it helps you remember what you are noticing. *(Take no more than 4 minutes to complete each drawing.)*

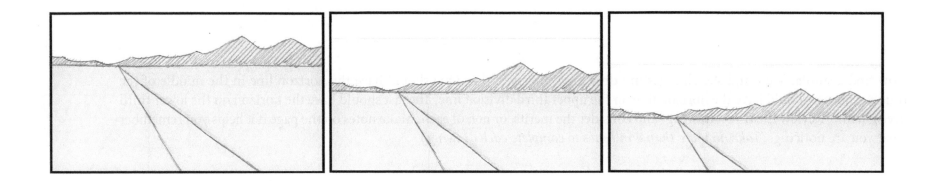

Exercise 42

Two-Shot Action

Now find two people who are talking with one another and sketch a single profile gesture drawing of them both at the top of the next blank page. Position one of the figures on the right-hand one-third line and the other on the left-side third line. Now beneath this draw 2 more views of the same shot—one from a three-quarter view seen from the left side and another from a three-quarter view from the right. Keep the two people approximately on the same one-third vertical lines, however. Lastly, under these sketch a fourth version of the shot, placing both characters anywhere you like within the frame. Consider which of the four views work best for you and why. Make notes on the page if it helps you remember what you are noticing. *(Take no more than 4 minutes to complete each drawing.)*

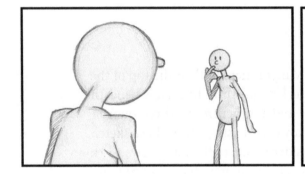 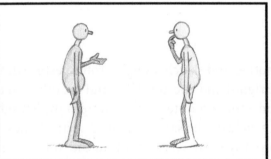 

Exercise 43

Reaction Shot

Now you need to observe and sketch a three-quarter medium shot of a person looking. (A medium shot is a shot of a figure seen from the waist to the top of her head.) The person should be somewhat in profile and needs to be looking from one side of the picture to the other. Sketch 2 versions of this on the next blank page. The first should have the character located on the right-side third line, and the other on the left-side third line. Consider the two and decide which one works best for the story intention of the shot. Make notes on the page if it helps you remember what you are noticing. *(Take no more than 3 minutes to complete each drawing.)*

Exercise 44

Person with Horizon

Finally, draw a figure from a back view as it looks away. Sketch 2 versions of this on the next blank page—one with the horizon beyond it on the lower one-third line of the shot and the other with the horizon on the upper one-third line. Consider the two versions and decide what different visual stories each is telling. Make notes on the page if it helps you remember what you are noticing. *(Take no more than 2 minutes to complete each drawing.)*

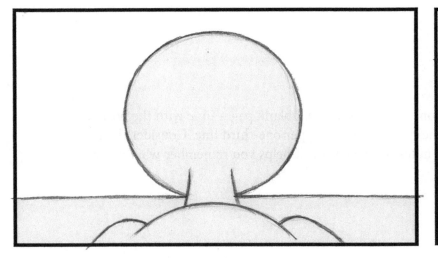

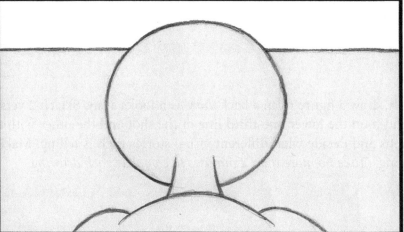

Exercise 45

Perspective

Perspective can often be incredibly important to animated action, in addition to shot construction. The farther away an object is, the smaller it will appear in the scene. The farther away a movement is in a scene, the slower it will appear to move. This is something that can be definitely exploited when animating. Perspective in backgrounds or environments also can be significantly dramatized—specifically to draw attention to where you want the audience's eye to focus. Animating in perspective can be very dramatic in other ways too. Therefore, on the understanding that the nearer an object or part of a person gets to the viewer, the larger it will appear, and vice versa, you can distort extremities accordingly. Animating backgrounds in perspective can provide some quite dramatic effects. So, go out and sketch on the next blank page examples of perspective and perspective manipulation that particularly appeal to you. Write notes beside your sketches to clarify why. *(Take no more than 5 minutes to create each sketch.)*

Exercise 46

One-Point Perspective

Perspective drawings can be drawn using three different viewpoint techniques: one-point perspective, two-point perspective, or three-point perspective. Here, we will start with one-point perspective. On the next blank page, draw a square that is positioned slightly to the left of frame center. Behind it, add a horizontal horizon line. Now, to add depth to the square and turn it into a cube in perspective, draw an angled line from the top of the right corner of the cube to somewhere along the horizon to the right. (Note: The point where this line dissects the horizon is called the vanishing point.) Draw a similar angled line from the bottom of the same side to the vanishing point on the horizon. Next, draw a vertical line somewhere away from the right side of the square that dissects both angled horizon lines to create a side to the square. Shade in the side to emphasize the cube's depth. You've now created a three-dimensional shape, in perspective, using one-point perspective. *(Take no more than 1 minute to complete this drawing.)*

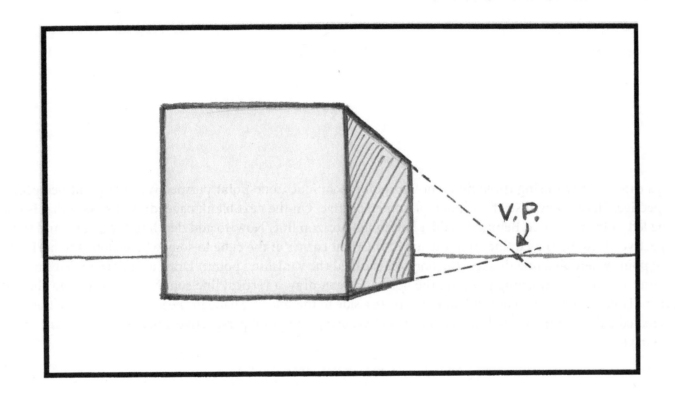

Exercise 47

Two-Point Perspective

On the next blank page, draw a vertical line representing the nearest corner of a cube that we'll be creating. Center this line within the frame. Add a horizon line behind it, as you did before in Exercise 46. Now draw angled lines from the top of the vertical line to points along the horizon on both sides of the corner line. These are also known as vanishing points. Draw similar dissecting lines from the bottom of the vertical line to the same two vanishing points. Add vertical side lines to the right and left of the vertical line to suggest the depth of the cube on both its sides. Shade one of these sides to imply depth. You have now created a three-dimensional shape, in perspective, using two-point perspective. *(Take no more than 2 minutes to complete this drawing.)*

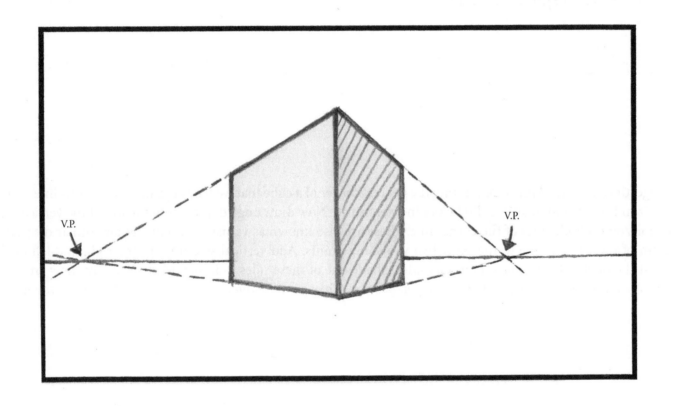

Exercise 48

Three-Point Perspective

Lightly draw a vertical center line from the top to the bottom of the frame. Mark a single point (A) approximately two-thirds of the way up the center line and another single point (B) about halfway from the top point to the bottom of the frame. These represent the top and bottom of the nearest edge of a cube we will create. Draw a horizon line just above the top point. Next, draw angled lines from the top edge point to two vanishing points on the horizon line either side of the center line (VP1 and VP2). Draw similar lines from the bottom point on the center line to the same (VP1 and VP2) vanishing points on the horizon. Next, create a new vanishing point (VP3) near the bottom of the center line and draw angled lines upward in both directions so they can describe the left and right sides of the cube. Now, draw a dissecting line from the top part of the cube's right-hand side (C) to the left-side vanishing point (VP1) on the horizon. Do the same for the cube's left-hand side (D) to the right-side vanishing point (VP2). Finally, draw a line from the bottom corner of the cube's right side (E) to the left horizon vanishing point (VP1) and a similar line from the bottom of the cube's left side (F) to the right horizon vanishing point (VP2). This will now define the three sides (i, ii, and iii), in perspective, of a three-dimensional cube using three-point perspective. To make the cube more apparent, thicken the lines that define its front, top, and side edges and shade in one side face to suggest the depth. *(Take no more than 4 minutes to complete this drawing.)*

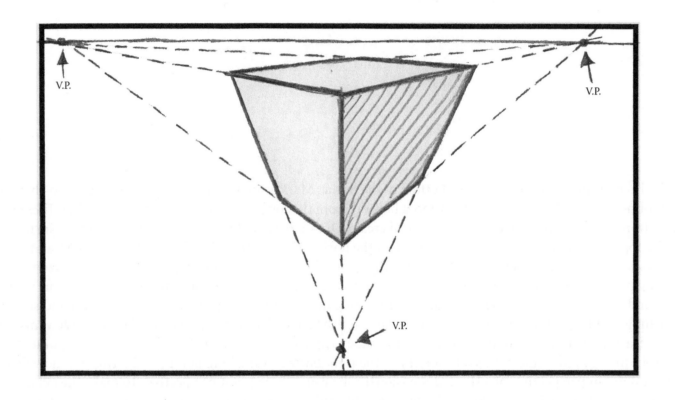

The Animator's Sketchbook

Exercise 49

Forced Figure Perspective

Now working more figuratively and less geometrically, sketch on the next blank page a character that is walking toward you. Next to it, draw an identical version of this figure pose, but this time exaggerate the perspective—meaning that the body parts nearest to you have to be drawn much larger, with the body parts farthest from you drawn significantly smaller. Compare the different visual effects between the two drawings. *(Take no more than 4 minutes to complete each drawing.)*

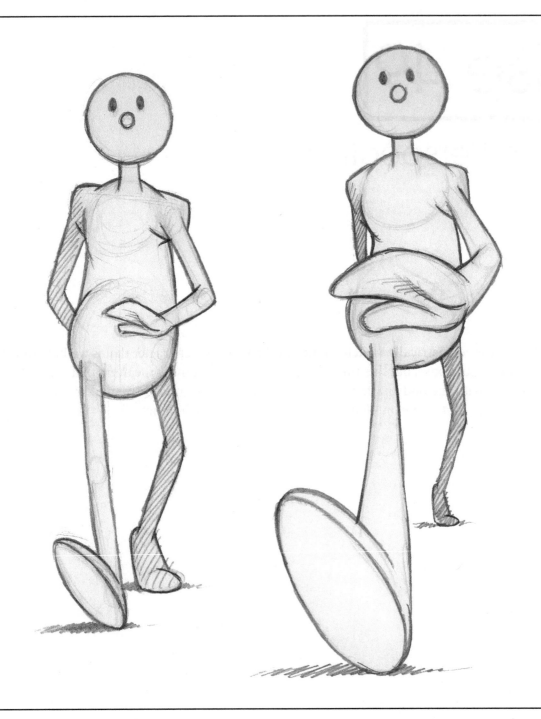

Exercise 50

Drawing Objects in Perspective

Finally, walking into the distance with perspective. On the next blank page, sketch out a scene in perspective where the farthest (smallest) part of the street is to the right of the frame and the nearest (largest) part to the left. Add a walking figure in full stride pose to the left (A) and a second drawing of the same character in a similar pose, but much smaller, to the right (B). Lightly draw in perspective lines between them both, i.e., from head to head and from feet to feet. Now, to calculate an accurately scaled half-way stride postion, in perspective, you need to lightly draw a line from the top of the head of one character to the bottom of the feet on the other. Then do a similar thing with a line from the feet of the first character to the head of the second. Where they intersect, that is the natural perspective center for a middle pose between the first two (C). This process can be repeated between any two character positions in perspective until all the required perspective keys are achieved. *(Take no more than 3 minutes to complete each figure drawing, although the street perspective drawing in the background will take longer of course.)*

(Note: This technique can be applied to drawn background elements too, such as telegraph poles alongside a railway track or lamp-posts in a street, ensuring there is a natural perspective feel throughout.)

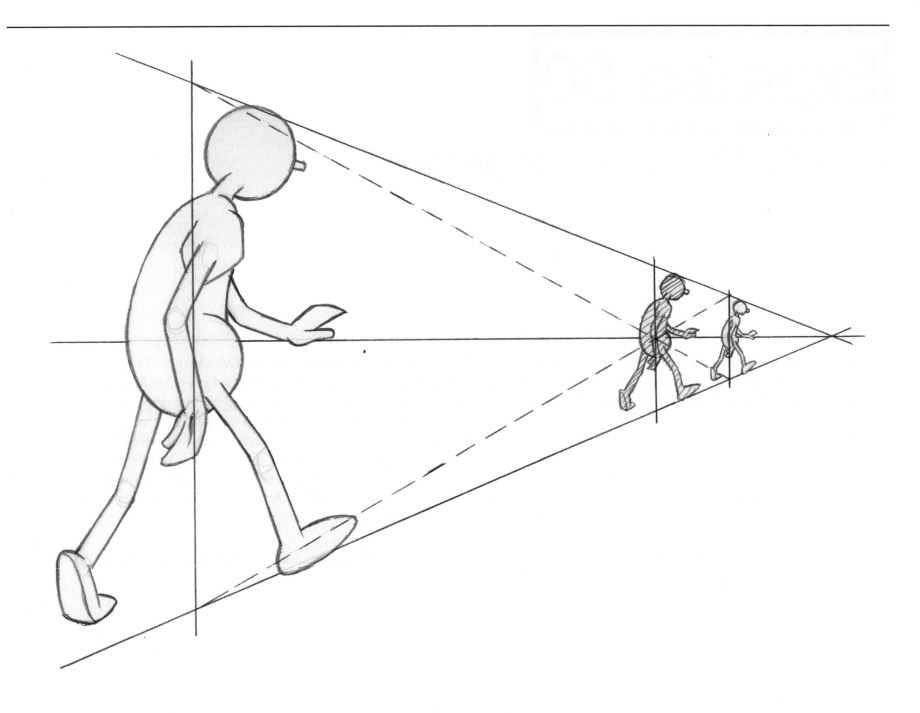

The Animator's Sketchbook

Exercise 51

Light and Shade

The use of light and shade can have a very dramatic effect on the way drawings—or animated sequences—are presented. The age-old saying that comes to mind here is "Light over dark, or dark over light." This means that when shading or coloring an image, make any foreground character you have appear light against a dark background, or dark against a light background. That will ensure it will appear stronger. This of course only maximizes the silhouette effect we worked with earlier. Another thing that is also good to remember here is that the eye is always drawn to the part of an image that has the strongest light and shade contrast. So, always remember to exploit this fact when you're featuring an important piece of animated action within a scene. Practically, to reinforce all this, research paintings, illustrations, and film clips and draw quick thumbnail sketches of the most effective images you find. Work fast, but do add both light and shading—and observational notes—to your work. This will prove an invaluable archive of ideas and information for future use. *(Take no more than 2 minutes per thumbnail drawing.)*

Exercise 52

Dark on Light

Now find a location near you that has a strong foreground element and which also has an interesting background scene behind it. On the next blank page, sketch the scene and then darkly shade the foreground element in it to emphasize it. Ensure that the foreground element makes a strong silhouette as you render it. *(Take no more than 5 minutes to complete this drawing.)*

Exercise 53

Light on Dark

Using the same location, shade the background but not the foreground. Make sure that your foreground element still stands out in contrast to the rendered background. Compare this drawing with your previous one and make notes on the page regarding the differences between both. *(Take no more than 5 minutes to complete this drawing.)*

Exercise 54

Light within Dark

Select a location to draw that has a pretty dark overall feel to it but contains a strong element of light within one part of it. Sketch what you see on the next blank page, but add a silhouetted figure or object in front of the light area. Silhouette it darkly, so it has a strong contrast to the light area. *(Take no more than 5 minutes to complete this drawing.)*

Exercise 55

Rim Lighting

Select a location with a mood similar to the one you drew in Exercise 54, but this time put a darkly silhouetted figure into a darker area of the background. However, highlight just some parts of the figure using rim lighting (i.e., light that reflects from the outer edges of a figure's outline to emphasize its contours against a darker background). Remember, though, that everything in the scene will also be influenced by the same light source that causes the rim lighting, although perhaps not so markedly. *(Take no more than 5 minutes to complete this drawing.)*

Exercise 56

Light Layers

Finally with light. Seek an outside location that has many layered elements that reach off into the distance. On the next blank page, draw and shade each of the layered elements differently (i.e., with either them getting lighter the farther they are seen away from the viewer, or else darker). If you have the time and inclination, sketch both options and compare. *(Take no more than 8 minutes to complete this drawing.)*

Exercise 57

Strength of Line

We should briefly mention in conclusion that strength of line can have an important part to play in visual communication. Strength of line means how thick or thin you make your lines when creating a drawing or illustration. For example, most drawings have an even line thickness all over, whether they are background or foreground objects being drawn. However, if you draw the foreground with a much thicker line, specifically the outline, then the foreground elements will tend to stick out from the background ones a little more. Sometimes, a single line can have a thick and thin element within it, which gives an entirely other effect. To familiarize yourself with different techniques, make some line thickness studies from other artists' work. Fill the next blank page with thumbnail sketches and notes you have arrived at when looking at a number of different cartoon, comic book, or illustration styles. *(Take no more than 3 minutes for each thumbnail drawing.)*

Exercise 58

Strong Foreground Line

On the next blank page, draw, from your imagination, 3 frames that contain a strong foreground line element but with an even line thickness throughout. *(Take no more than 3 minutes to complete this drawing.)*

Exercise 59

Thicker Outline

Now draw the same 3 frames again on the next blank page. However, this time thicken the lines around the outside of the foreground element. Note how this time the foreground element really stands out against the background and has more visual impact. *(Take no more than 5 minutes to complete this drawing.)*

Exercise 60

Storyboarding

Storyboarding is something that most animators will need to do at some stage in their career, especially those who are making animated films. It's possible that you may not be required to create a formal storyboard for a film ultimately, but you will certainly be well advised to do a quick thumbnail storyboard of any animation sequence you're about to create. Understanding of basic language of film is valuable here, as without having that kind of vocabularly, it's going to be hard for you to find your voice. We'll deal with that in a minute, however. First, to give you some kind of comparison, you need to create a quick storyboard *before* you learn the rules of filmmaking. Using about 6 frames on the next blank page, visualize and sketch out the story of a cowboy riding across a desert and suddenly being spooked by a rattlesnake that's glaring at him. Once you've done that, we'll walk you through a generic, classically-structured, more formulaic way of doing the same thing. *(Take no more than 5 minutes to rough out your storyboard frames.)*

Exercise 61

Extreme Wide Establishing Shot

There are a number of generic shots in filmmaking that an animated filmmaker can take advantage of when seeking to tell a strong filmic story. For our cowboy scenario, we'll go over the most basic of these here, beginning with the extremely wide establishing shot. So, on the next blank page draw the first frame, which is a view of a wide and most expansive part of a hot, barren desert. It might show distant hills or mountains, or it might be just a flat horizon. There could even be a few cacti littering the scene way into the distance. But whatever you draw, try to get over the feeling of a huge landscape that dwarfs any human content. Use reference to guide you. *(Take no more than 3 minutes to complete this drawing.)*

(Note: For a wider understanding of film language, refer to the section in the Appendix at the end of this book. This will prove valuable to you as you move forward in creating more sophisticated storyboards as time goes by.)

Exercise 62

Wide Shot

This frame requires you to draw the audience into the scene a little more, providing more detail of the desert and its contents. It's still a wide shot, but now that it's somewhat closer, you need to indicate the tiny, dark silhouette of the cowboy on a horse riding toward the viewer. *(Take no more than 3 minutes to complete this drawing on the next blank page.)*

Exercise 63

Medium Shot

Now we draw in even closer. Therefore, you should draw the cowboy on his horse, framed from his stomach area to the top of his hat. This medium shot should give the audience more visual information on the cowboy as he approaches, and your drawing should definitely suggest to us that he is most definitely a tough guy. Also, with the cowboy filling much more of the scene, now you won't need to draw so much of the landscape detail behind him. *(Take no more than 3 minutes to complete this drawing.)*

Exercise 64

Close-up Shot

The close-up shot brings the audience even closer to our subject's face. Framing-wise, you now need to draw just his head and hat filling the frame, with very little of the landscape behind him being visible. The closeness of this shot will give the audience more information about our cowboy, such as the fact that a bead of sweat is clearly running down from his forehead to his cheek in the heat. *(Take no more than 3 minutes to complete this drawing.)*

Exercise 65

Extreme Close-up Shot

Finally, we feature only the cowboy's cheek filling the frame as his finger wipes the sweat from it. Being so close in, we might only now notice other details about him, such as the fact that there is a jagged old scar on one of our cowboy's cheeks. Your drawing should also confirm that this is clearly a very tough hombre. Alternatively, you could cut away to an extreme close-up shot of what the cowboy is seeing—maybe another cowboy's finger on the trigger of a gun, or the glaring eye of a snake as it is about to strike! *(Take no more than 3 minutes to complete this drawing.)*

Exercise 66

Final Storyboarding Exercise

Now that you have a sense of shot selection to dramatize story action, create a short storyboard sequence using the blank frames that follow. Taking your best shot at storytelling, share a significant moment in your own life—as if you were going to film it. Your story can be happy, sad, frightening, hilarious, indeed anything that has been especially significant to you. Select and draw your shots wisely and frame each image in accordance with everything you've learned throughout this book. Ultimately, you should be able to defend and justify every shot or framing choice you make, as you would need to do in a professional context anyway. (Note: There is no time limit to this exercise, although each frame should still be created with speed drawing sketching techniques.)

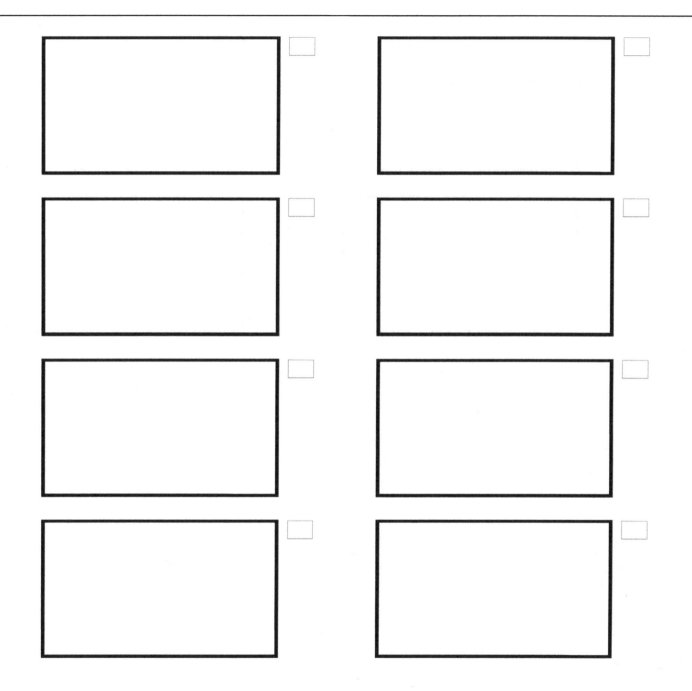

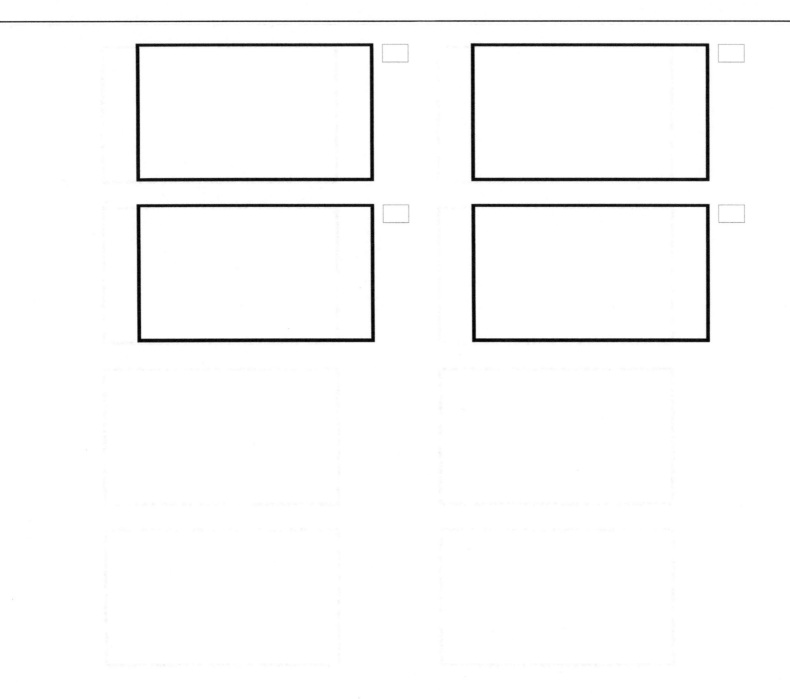

PART 3
Appendix

Part 3

Appendix

Turnaround Arnie Model Sheet

Before animators bring a character to life—especially traditional hand-drawn animators, but also CG film and game character designers—a turnaround model sheet has to be created. A turnaround model sheet shows the character to be animated from every angle, so that every visual aspect of that character is known before it is worked with.

The following image is an Arnie turnaround model sheet I created to help me understand how the character works when seen from most angles. The reason that I created Arnie decades ago for my animation students is simply because he is simple to draw, which is something traditional 2D animation students especially are grateful for when they attempt to animate the exercises I give them. (Note: It is hard enough to work through exercises in movement, quite apart from stuggling to draw a difficult character at the same time.)

This particular turnaround model sheet looks a little formal at this stage. However, it will perhaps give students working with this book a simple-to-draw, yet well-structured character to work with in a speed drawing situation. You might choose to go with your own character of course, but this will be a safe start for you—and Arnie is still a character I use when going out and sketching pose reference for my own animation work.

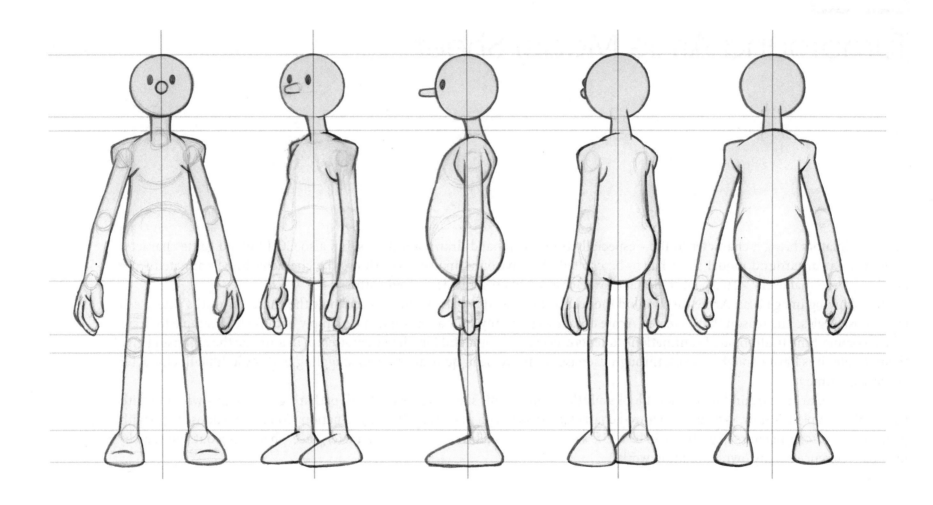

The Animator's Sketchbook

Try the Arnie Approach for Yourself

You may find that using Arnie for the assignments in this book frees you up from other pressures. For example, by working with someone else's character that has been fully lab tested over the years, you will be able to better study the material without having to worry about creating a character design of your own that stands up to all the visual challenges you will face. Arnie really is fast and basic to draw, and as pose and gesture are the objectives within this book's process, perhaps his minimalist approach is the easiest one to take for your sketching—short of a basic stick figure, that is. To find out how he works for you, sketch all three views on the graph guide on the next page. When you have your three Arnie poses complete, you might try to add the three-quarter front and three-quarter back views too. At the end of all that, you will certainly know if Arnie is the character of drawing choice for you.

Design Your Own Personal Arnie Character

Having drawn my Arnie for yourself, perhaps you will now feel that he is not for you. If so, it's time to create your own alternative character. On the next page, sketch out some thumbnail design ideas for a character of your own. Don't be too detailed with it at this stage. Brainstorm ideas of shapes, styles, and forms. However, do bear in mind that what you will eventually arrive at must be simple and fast to draw, due to the speed drawing nature of the majority of the exercises in this sketchbook. Always remember, *simple is best.*

Your Own Character Turnaround Model Sheet

Now that you've created many thumbnail ideas for your own Arnie character, select the one you most favor and, on the next page, create a formal turnaround model sheet of it. Once you've done this, you should stick with your character throughout this entire sketchbook program, so you get to really know and understand working with it.

(Tip: Choose your character well and choose it wisely. Time yourself when drawing each of the character views on your own model sheet too. That way, you'll know if you'll be able to draw it within the 2–5 minutes that most of this sketchbook's assignments will require you to draw it in.)

Film Language

I am totally convinced that pretty much all the information contained in this sketchbook so far will be of enormous value to you on your journey to animation mastery. However, from a storytelling or storyboarding point of view, there is a little more information on film language that you might want at your disposal. I liken this to an artist having a palette of color options to choose from when attempting a painting. Film has its own palette of options, and here are 3 more of them.

Shots

Shots are the methods of framing a shot to tell a specific story. (Note: We have dealt with shot options earlier in the sketchbook, but this is a brief recap of what we have touched on, plus some extra thoughts about them.)

Ultrawide shot: This offers an extreme (often spectacular or overwhelming) panoramic shot that will set the scene for later options. Often, this is so wide a shot that there is rarely little chance of seeing a person or an object within the scale of the view being featured. This is usually a breathtaking opening sequence shot that establishes where the unfolding story will take place (an "establishing shot").

Wide shot: This is similar to the ultrawide shot in that it is also a scene-setting establishing shot option. However, as it is not quite so extreme in its scale, it is more able to also feature a focal point in the shot at the same time, such as a person, car, or train.

Medium shot: This is used if requiring a person to be the prime focus of the scene. It approximately frames him from the waistline upward, to the top of his head.

Close-up shot: This shot really draws us into the feature or emotions of a central character. It usually frames a character from her neck to the top of her head. If the face is not a feature of the action, however, the shot closely features another part of the body or another object.

Extreme close-up: This shot features a minute detail within a specific part of a face, body, etc., within a scene. It is used especially to share a specific piece of information, or close-up action, with the audience.

Transitions

The methods of moving from shot to shot throughout a sequence.

Cut: This is where one scene immediately transitions to another over one frame. This is a transition used most of the time by all filmmakers.

Dissolve (also known as a mix): This is a transition that takes place over a number of frames, i.e., where one scene is fading out over that number of frames while the next scene is fading in simultaneously. This kind of transition often implies a slight change in time or a softening of transition in some way.

Fade-out: A fade-out occurs when an outgoing scene simply drifts away—usually to black. It can indicate that a scene is finished but the director wants the audience to linger on it a little while longer. It can also imply a longer changing of time or a momentary pause before the next scene begins.

Fade-up: This is when an incoming scene slowly appears over a period of frames, usually emerging from black to a full exposure. It is a gentle way of introducing a new sequence to the audience, or to indicate the end of a passing in time (especially if it follows a fade-out from the previous scene).

Wipe: This is where an invisible line crosses the screen—erasing the first outgoing scene from view and revealing the next incoming scene as it does so. It is pretty much an old-school approach to transitions, but it can be very effective in a retro style of filmmaking. Wipes can range from a single straight line to complex shapes or spirals of transitioning action.

Continuity

The rules of ensuring that there is no confusion in the minds of the audience about what is happening from scene to scene. Here are two critical ones.

1. If a character exits screen right in one shot, he needs to enter from screen left in the next, to keep the line of action moving along the same plane.
2. If two people are seen interacting during a number of scenes—with one positioned to the right and the other positioned to the left—they need to maintain that relationship throughout a sequence of subsequent shots. If they do not do this, the audience will be confused—on a subconscious level, if nothing else—and an important line of dialogue or action could be missed while the audience is trying to adjust to the sudden change of continuity.

Last Thoughts

At the beginning of this sketchbook, I suggest that drawing from life is the finest way of seeing and understanding what you are attempting, or about to attempt. I hope nothing you have since read in this book has changed your mind on this—it certainly hasn't changed my mind in writing it. However, there are quite often circumstances where drawing from life is just not possible. For example, you may be animating a sporting action or a ballet sequence and it's just not possible for you to be there in person to sketch what is happening. Consequently, my advice to you is move on to the next best possibility and work from there.

If you cannot possibly view action reference "live," then your next best thing would be to film yourself or someone else acting out the movement for you. That way you'll get the precise action you need on tape and can forever observe it—freeze framing as you go—when you need to.

If videotaping is not possible, then go online and view a video of something similar to what you want that has already been filmed. You can then adapt this to your needs as required.

If online film is not available, then perhaps Google Images will at least give you some frozen key pose positions of the action or at least something close to it.

The very last thing you want to do, however, is draw from your imagination—at least at the action research stage. Imagination is wonderful for origination of ideas, but when you need to practically put those ideas into practice, you should research any and all visual references you can to find how things actually do work and move.

If you are actually animating something that doesn't exist in the real world anyway, you can rely on imagination to some extent of course. But even then, do go to the nearest possible reference you can find and base your judgment and animation approach on this. For example, if you need to animate a dragon, find film footage of the nearest lizard or snake that somewhat looks like your dragon design and sketch out those movements for yourself. These will provide you with a great number of clues as to how your fantasy dragon might plausibly move in your fantasy piece.

By all means be creative in your imaginings, especially at the concept stage. This is what the world of animation is all about. But then go to the best reference source available to you to get the mechanics of movement right. In the long run, all these additional efforts will be greatly rewarded and you'll be well on your way to that animation mastership that everyone aspires to.

Tony White

Animator's Sketchclub

Readers of this book might like to be part of the author's online Animator's Sketchclub. Each month an animation-related drawing challenge is set for anyone who is keen to improve their basic observational skills and share what they see by drawing it. Challenges are varied and have proven extremely popular with many of the thousands of members who have joined the group. Final challenge submissions are posted to a private Facebook group page, where the winner of each challenge and the runners up have his or her work displayed on the www.animatorssketchclub.com 'Gallery' page. That said, the Animator's Sketchclub is not a competitive group. Indeed, members are very supportive of each other and respectful of everyone's work—whether drawings are submitted by raw beginner or master professional.

ANIMATOR'S SKETCHCLUB

HOME // CHALLENGES // GALLERY // CONTACT

A DRAWING COMMUNITY FOR ANIMATION ARTISTS OF ALL KINDS

ABOUT

With the ceaseless march of technology it is easy to forget the value of traditional art skills in animation – especially *drawing*! The **Animator's Sketchclub** is a place where animators of all kinds can get back to their traditional drawing roots and learn how to '**see**' and how to '**interpret**' what they see for animation – just like the great *Masters* of the past did! The **ANIMATOR'S SKETCHCLUB** is also a place where artists can simply let their hair down and just have '*fun*' learning how to be a better animator!

CHALLENGES

To assist in the *seeing* and *interpreting* process we offer a FREE monthly **DRAWING CHALLENGE**, so that animation artists can draw and submit to us online. The best entries from each month's challenge will be featured on our **GALLERY PAGE** as well as on our private **FACEBOOK PAGE** – with constructive comments and feedback included wherever possible Note To post your monthly Challenge drawings *(and only those those I'm afraid)* – you have to apply to become a **Facebook Group** member!

ANIMATOR'S SKETCHBOOK

The ***ANIMATOR'S SKETCHBOOK*** is inspired by the new workbook, written by master animator, **Tony White**. Taking well over a year to prepare *(and over 4 decades of top professional experience to know!)* Tony's new book – "**The ANIMATOR'S SKETCHBOOK**" – contains **60** well-conceived drawing assignments that will help animators of all persuasion to '**see**', '**interpret**' and '**communicate**' their animation poses better. To find out more about the unique "***ANIMATOR'S SKETCHBOOK***, click the link HERE!

Drawing the way of the Masters before us!

DRAWTASTIC Festival of Drawing & Animation

Author **Tony White** is passionate about seeing a return of top quality 2D animation production in the USA. Since the closure of Disney's traditional animation studio in 2002 and the advance of our increasingly digitally-obsessive age, the professional art-form of hand-crafted 2D animation is in danger of being lost forever. This is a terrible tragedy as America once led the world in this particular field. Therefore, to encourage a renaissance of traditional 2D animation in the USA once more Tony has devised a two-fold plan. 'Part A' of this plan is to once again raise the consciousness of traditional art and animation in America. 'Plan B' is to encourage a viable 2D production industry once more—at least at the 'indie' production level if nothing else. Consequently the major part of 'Plan A' is the creation of the **DRAWTASTIC Festival of Drawing & Animation**. The festival, successfully launched on April 30, 2016 in Seattle, fundamentally supports all forms of animation—but especially so for traditional hand-drawn animation. Filmmakers from all over the world submit their work to DRAWTASTIC's '2D OR NOT 2D' event, each vying for one of Tony's coveted '**Golden Pencil Awards**'. Top-level speakers from all aspects of the creative world—each having an allegiance to the 'humble pencil'—also come to teach and conduct workshops at the event. DRAWTASTIC is an annual event, so all interested artists and filmmakers should visit the festival website at **www.drawtastic.org** for further information. It's 'Pencil Power' at its very best!

Resources

Recommended Drawing Books for Animators

Drawn to Life by Walt Stanchfield, Volumes 1 and 2 (Focal Press)
Pose Drawing Sparkbook by Cedric Hohnstadt (Sparkbook Publishing)

Tony White's Books for Animators

The Animator's Workbook (Phaidon Press)
Animation from Pencils to Pixels (Focal Press)
How to Make Animated Films (Focal Press)
The Animator's Notebook (Focal Press)

Tony White's iBooks for Animators

Motion Comics (DRAWASSIC on iTunes)
Drawn Together, a compilation of work by 222 different animators/artists in support of traditional, hand-drawn animation (DRAWASSIC on iTunes)

Self-Published by Tony White

The Animator's Job Coach (DRAWASSIC on Lulu.com)

About the Author

Tony White is a British Academy Award-winning animation director, animator, author, educator and mentor. At the beginning of his career, he studied classical animation techniques with some of the finest masters of the art-form, specifically—Ken Harris (original lead animator of "Bugs Bunny," "Roadrunner," etc.), Art Babbitt (original lead animator on *Pinocchio, Fantasia,* etc.) and apprenticed with Richard Williams (3-time Oscar winner and author of *The Animator's Survival Kit*). Tony is currently Program Director & Senior Instructor of the Academy of Interactive Entertainment's 'Skills Center' program and is founder/CEO of DRAWASSIC, a new initiative that seeks to preserve, teach and evolve the art-form of traditional animation in this digital age. DRAWASSIC is currently developing a number of original indie animation projects, as well as hosting the groundbreaking 'DRAWTASTIC Festival of Drawing and Animation' in Seattle. Tony's best-selling animation books include: *The Animator's Workbook; Animation from Pencils to Pixels—Classical Techniques for Digital Animators; How to Make Animated Films, Jumping through Hoops: The Animation Job Coach* and *The Animator's Notebook*. Tony is currently developing his own online program in animation, to be launched under the title of the Animation Grail. This program will offer comprehensive foundational training for all students of animation, whether their interest be 2D, 3D or any other kind. Tony's free online ANIMATOR'S SKETCHCLUB group currently exceeds over 6,000 members at the time of this book's publication!

T - #0338 - 101024 - C0 - 216/279/18 [20] - CB - 9781138418226 - Gloss Lamination